THE
DEMETER
STAR

A.F. ORESHNIK

A Pacemaker® Book

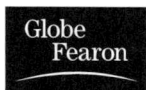

Globe
Fearon

Upper Saddle River, New Jersey
www.globefearon.com

The PACEMAKER® BESTSELLERS™

Bestellers I

Diamonds in the Dirt
Night of the Kachina
The Verlaine Crossing
Silvabamba
The Money Game

Flight to Fear
The Time Trap
The Candy Man
Three Mile House
Dream of the Dead

Bestellers II

Black Beach
Crash Dive
Wind Over Stonehenge
Gypsy
Escape from Tomorrow

The Demeter Star
North to Oak Island
So Wild a Dream
Wet Fire
Tiger, Lion, Hawk

Bestellers III

Star Gold
Bad Moon
Jungle Jenny
Secret Spy
Little Big Top

The Animals
Counterfeit!
Night of Fire and Blood
Village of Vampires
I Died Here

Bestellers IV

Dares
Welcome to Skull Canyon
Blackbeard's Medal
Time's Reach
Trouble at Catskill Creek

The Cardiff Hill Mystery
Tomorrow's Child
Hong Kong Heat
Follow the Whales
A Changed Man

Series Director: Tom Belina
Designer: Richard Kharibian
Cover and illustrations: Warren Lee

ISBN: 0-822-45270-7

Library of Congress Catalog Card Number: 77-77157
Printed in the United States of America.
6 7 8 9 10   05 04 03 02 01

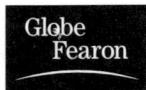

Globe
Fearon

1-800-848-9500
www.globefearon.com

CONTENTS

CHAPTER 1

MEREK'S MARINE MARKET

Mike Hatcher climbed down from the bus and let his bag drop to his feet. He was not tall, but he was not small, either. He had a wide back and thick arms. He looked strong enough to finish any job he started.

A bright sun was high in the afternoon sky. He could feel its heat through his shirt. The door of the bus closed behind him with a bang. Then the bus pulled away, filling the air with brown, blowing dust.

Mike held his breath. He didn't want to fill his lungs with dirty air. After the bus was gone, he took a deep breath. It was great! He could smell the ocean. That was something he had not been able to do on the bus. Even when he could see the water, he couldn't smell it. The bus windows could not be opened.

Mike looked around. His eyes were a light blue, like the old Levi's he had on. *Vista Del Mar, California,* a sign said. *Population: 1523.*

It seemed bigger than a town with only 1523 people. There seemed to be too many stores and homes. Mike decided the 1523 must be the people who lived there all year. But a lot of people came just for the summer to spend their vacations there.

Vista Del Mar was on the side of a hill. From where he stood, Mike could see many large homes below him. Also, a line of beach houses, a wide strip of yellow sand, and the ocean. This "view of the sea" must have been what gave the town its name.

The bus had let Mike off at the end of a line of businesses. They were on both sides of the road. There was a gas station, a small hotel, an eating place, and several stores. Many of the stores sold sports equipment.

Mike didn't know where to start. But he had to begin somewhere, so he picked up his bag. He headed for the gas station.

There was a young man about Mike's age. He was standing outside the station office, holding a bottle of Pepsi Cola. Mike walked over to him.

"Hi!" Mike said. "You run this place?"

"No, I just work here."

"Who do I see about a job?" Mike asked.

"This is Mr. Jackson's station. He will be back in a couple of hours. But, there isn't much chance he will give you a job."

"Why not?"

"You just got off the bus. He doesn't like to take on anyone who hasn't lived here at least six months."

"Why is that?" Mike wanted to know.

"Because there have been a lot of people who worked for a few weeks, then left. They had come here for a vacation, not really to work. He figures a person has to have lived here six months or so. Then he might take a chance on him. He doesn't want to spend time showing people how he wants things done, then have them leave."

Mike pointed toward the other businesses. "Does everyone feel that way?"

The man took a drink of Pepsi and wiped his mouth with the back of his hand. "Yes, I think so," he answered.

That was bad news. Mike had hoped he could find a job as soon as he got to Vista Del Mar. He had thought a vacation spot would have plenty of work. Now it looked like he couldn't have been more wrong.

That was the worst kind of news. All he had was about five dollars in his pocket. That wasn't even enough to buy a bus ticket to the next big city. He had to find a job soon.

But Mike wasn't worried. He didn't worry about the future because he didn't fear it. He took each day as it came and made the most of it.

At the same time, he didn't just sit back and wait for good things to happen. He knew that the only way to have good luck was to help it along. He knew he had to give good luck a chance to happen.

So he looked up the street and picked out another business. The Vista Del Mar Hotel looked good to him. He picked up his bag and started walking.

At the hotel, Mike was listened to, but he wasn't given a job. They didn't want anyone who was new in town. It was the same story as at the gas station.

Mike picked up his bag and returned to the street. This time he studied the signs a lot longer. Then he headed across the street to Merek's Marine Market.

From the distance, Mike had thought the store sold things for boats. He was wrong. When he reached the store, he stopped long enough to look through the window. It was filled with swimming and diving equipment. There were swim fins, air tanks, and many other things used by divers.

Mike pushed open the door and went inside. There were two people in the store. One was a tall, thin man not many years older than Mike. The other was a very pretty girl. She had bright yellow hair. Mike could tell by the way they stood and watched him walk toward them that they must run the place.

"Can I help you?" the thin man asked. "I'm Ed Merek."

"I'm looking for a job," Mike said. "Do you need someone to help out around here?"

"Maybe," Ed Merek said. "The busy season is just starting. Do you know anything about diving?"

"Sure," Mike lied. "I know *all* about it."

"Nobody knows all about it," Ed said.

Mike made a face. "Caught again," he said. "Why is it I can never tell a lie without being found out?"

The girl smiled, showing even, white teeth. "Maybe it's because you're no good at telling lies," she said. Then she added, "I'm Carol Vinton, a friend of Ed's. I also help out in the shop when I can."

"Mike Hatcher," Mike said, holding out his hand to the girl. "My friends call me Hatch."

Carol shook his hand, then Ed did, too. Ed said, "You need a job, do you? Why did you pick Vista Del Mar? And why did you pick this store?"

"I came to Vista Del Mar because I thought I might find interesting work," Mike answered. "And I picked this store because, so far, no one else would have me."

Ed smiled. "For someone who started out lying, you sure got honest in a hurry. How bad do you need a job?"

"I'm down to my last five dollars," Mike said.

"Then you need a job, all right. And I need some help. The trouble is, this is a new store. All my money is tied up in the equipment I have for sale. It may be months before I could pay you

very much." He stopped talking for a second. Then he said, "I may never be able to pay you very much."

"Now who is being honest?" Mike said.

"Well, I thought you should know where I stand," Ed said. "Now, let me ask you about diving again. Have you ever done any scuba diving?"

"No," Mike answered.

"Good," Ed said. "Then I can make diving lessons a part of your pay. You're lucky. You won't have any wrong moves to try to forget. You can learn the right way the first time. I have a training pool behind the store. When do you want to get started?"

"Does this mean I have a job?"

"Sure," Ed said. "Where else will I find a man who needs me as much as I need him? Years from now you'll remember me as the man who taught you to dive for treasure."

"Treasure? Did you say 'dive for treasure'?"

"Yes, I did."

Mike smiled. "In that case, we can get started right now," he said.

"OK, drop your bag and come with me," Ed told him.

CHAPTER **2**

FIRST TIME OUT

Ed Merek led the way through the store. In the rear, as he had said, there was a pool. It was 20 feet square and 15 feet deep.

"There is one rule you must always remember," Ed said. "Never dive alone. That's true for this training pool, too. Never come back here unless someone is with you."

"Isn't scuba diving safe?" Mike asked.

"Yes, it is. It's one of the safest sports there is. But it's never smart to take chances you don't have to take. And it's only safe if you know what you're doing."

"OK," Mike said. "What do we do first?"

"First we find some equipment for you. Then I'm going to teach you not to be afraid of the water."

Ed got a pair of red swim trunks for Mike and told him where he could change into them.

Then he gave him a face mask and a snorkel. The snorkel was a bent tube that let Mike breathe while his face was underwater.

"Don't I get an air tank?" Mike asked.

"Later," Ed said. "You have to learn to walk before you can learn to run."

Ed taught Mike how to breathe and use his fins. He taught him how to use just his fins to move forward. At first, Mike had wanted to use his arms to swim with, too. But Ed explained that using your arms was just a waste of power. Fins alone were better.

An hour went by in what seemed like minutes to Mike. Then Ed ended the lesson.

"That was fun," Mike said. "And I learned a lot, too."

"You'll learn even more tomorrow," Ed said.

"Can't we keep going? Or do you have to leave?"

"No, I don't have to leave. I saw you were getting tired."

"I am a little tired. But I don't mind staying here if you don't," Mike said.

"But I do mind," Ed told him. "That brings us to another rule you have to remember— *always* rest when you get tired. Stop to rest as often as you have to. Soon you'll know how to rest in the water. But for now, the best thing for us to do is end the lesson."

"OK," Mike said with a smile. "You're the man who knows."

"Don't ever forget that," Ed said.

As Ed had said, he couldn't pay very much. So, besides the diving lessons, he said he would lower the cost of any equipment Mike might buy. Also, he let Mike have a room in his house.

Ed Merek's house was on the beach. There were many new beach houses near it, but Merek's wasn't new. It looked like it had been there a long time. The paint was coming off in some places. The wood steps needed fixing, too.

"My grandfather first came to this beach when he was a young man," Ed said. "My family has come here for their summer vacations for as long as anyone can remember. It used to be one of the few beaches that didn't have a crowd.

"Now that a lot of people come here, I decided to stay here all year and open a store. Scuba diving is something I know well. And a lot of people are interested in it. This seems like the right business for me."

Mike helped in the store. He was needed most when Ed was away giving lessons. Then, there was too much work for Carol to handle alone. Mike learned fast. At first, he couldn't answer very many questions people asked him about diving equipment. If he had to know something, he would ask Carol. <u>But</u> after a while, he didn't need to ask as many questions.

Ed gave him diving lessons every day. After a few weeks, Mike wondered why he didn't get a chance to dive in deep water.

"Because most of the diving you do will be in water only about as deep as this training pool," Ed said. He explained that the best diving is in water about 15 to 35 feet deep. "A diver can stay down a long time and there is plenty of light from the sun. If you go deep, you can't stay down as long. If you do, gas bubbles build up in your blood. Then you have to come up very slowly or you can get the bends." Ed explained that the bends could kill you or cause you to never be able to walk again.

"And there is less light when you dive deep," Carol said. "The bright colors all seem to turn gray 40 or 50 feet down."

"What about the treasure you said I was going to dive for?" Mike asked.

"Everything you find in the ocean will be a treasure to you," Ed said.

"Oh, that's what you meant. I thought you knew where a treasure ship had gone down."

"No, I don't. But don't let me stop you from looking. That's half the fun of scuba diving. You never know what you will find, or where you will find it."

"Do you think I'm ready to dive in the ocean?"

"You're ready. How would you like to go spearfishing off White Rock Point? Carol and I are going after I close the store today."

"Great!" Mike said.

At closing time, they carried their equipment out to Ed's van. He had the rear fixed up like a home on wheels. There was a stove, running water, and just about everything else Ed might have wanted.

"I sometimes go diving down in Mexico," Ed told Mike. "With my van, I can just park and head for the water. My home is with me no matter where I go."

Ed parked and they carried their equipment to the beach. They had put on rubber wet suits before they left. The ocean water off California is very cold. They would need the wet suits to stay warm. Then they put on their fins and air tanks.

In a few minutes, they were walking to the water. "Be careful," Ed said. "The tide is going out. There may be some strong currents." They were walking backwards toward the water and looking silly. But walking backwards was the best way to walk with swim fins on. They looked silly on land. But when they lay down in the water, they moved like three large fish.

Mike swam out, away from the beach. Then he went down and floated along the bottom. He followed a few fish, but didn't try to spear any. This was great! He would never have believed how much fun diving was.

Suddenly, he felt himself being pulled away from the beach at high speed. He was caught in a current. He tried to swim out of it, but the current was too strong. He stopped trying to fight it. Ed had told him the ocean is too strong to fight. A smart diver doesn't try; he goes with it. Mike did just that.

Mike knew his air tank was saving his life. If he hadn't had it on, he would have drowned. Not that he wasn't in a lot of trouble. If the current didn't let him go until he was far out to sea, he might not be able to get back.

CHAPTER **3**

THE FIND

Mike rested while the current carried him. He remembered what Ed had told him about getting tired. He knew he might need all the power he had, so he didn't fight the water.

Then he saw something sticking up from the sea bottom. It was almost as big around as a telephone pole. He swam hard so that he could get his arms around it. Then he hung on.

After a few minutes the force of the current became less. Mike was able to swim to the surface and look around. He was far out to sea. From where he was, the people on the beach were tiny dots.

He was no longer worried about getting back. If he could see the beach, he could swim to it. Now he wanted to know about the pole that had saved him. He had a good idea what it was, but he wanted to be sure.

He dived until he found the pole again. He almost missed it. Its top was over 20 feet down. Then he began to follow it to the bottom.

He was right—it was the mast of a ship. There on the dark bottom was an old ship. It had broken in half. The front half was almost covered with sand and mud. The rear part was sitting on the bottom with the mast sticking up. It looked like a small cargo ship of some kind. The mast wasn't meant to hold sails. The ship had engines and was made of metal, not wood.

Mike turned and started swimming toward the surface. The mast was about 60 feet tall. And its tip was 20 feet from the surface. That meant the sea bottom where the ship rested was almost a hundred feet under the water.

Mike slowed down. He went up only as fast as the air bubbles from his mouth piece. He had not gone all the way to the bottom. And he had not been down long. Still, he knew he could get the bends if he came up too fast.

Once he reached the surface, Mike swam toward shore. Every time he kicked his feet, his fins pushed him forward with more speed. He covered the space to the beach in 20 minutes.

Ed and Carol were waiting for him.

"Where have you been?" Carol asked. "You had us worried sick."

"I got caught by the current," Mike said. "It took me out to sea."

"Yes, there is always the chance of that happening when the tide is going out," Ed said. "You were lucky you didn't end up half way to Hawaii."

"I might have," Mike said. "But I found something to hang on to."

"Found something to hang on to?" Ed said. "What could you have found out there?" He pointed to the ocean where the red California sun was going down.

"A ship," Mike said. "The mast of one, at least, I didn't find the ship until I followed the mast down to it."

"Are you trying to tell us you found a ship the first time you dived in the ocean?" Ed had a small smile on his lips. It was like he didn't believe Mike.

Mike's neck got red. "I'm not *trying* to tell you anything. I *am* telling you. I found an old ship out there."

"OK, OK, I believe you," Ed said, holding his hands in the air to show he gave up. "Do you think you can find it again?"

"I *know* I can find it again," Mike said. "I was careful to fix the spot in my mind. It's in line with this point of land and about half a mile out. It won't be hard to find."

"What kind of ship was it?" Carol asked.

"I don't know," Mike said. "It was pretty dark down there. The sun was getting low. And the ship was down almost a hundred feet. I didn't follow the mast all the way to the ship. I just went far enough to see it."

"Then maybe it wasn't a ship," Ed said. "The rocks on the bottom sometimes look like ships."

"Maybe they do," Mike said. "But I'll bet you have never seen a rock with a mast."

"No, I haven't," Ed said.

"Well," Carol said. "It's decided—Mike found a ship. Now what? Do we just stand around and talk about it? Or are we going to go out and take a look?"

"We should probably wait until tomorrow," Ed said. "It's going to be dark soon, but—"

"But?" Mike asked.

Ed smiled. "I have a rubber raft in my van and a pair of underwater lights. It's no use having those things if I don't use them."

CHAPTER **4**

NIGHT DIVE

Ed filled his raft with air. Then they put it into the water and started rowing. When Mike thought they were near the spot where he had seen the ship, they stopped.

"It's right about here," Mike said.

But two hours later, they still had not found it. Ed and Mike hung onto the side of the raft, resting. Carol sat, looking at them.

"If we don't find it pretty soon, we should stop," Ed said. "We have spent a lot of time in the water. And we have been deep most of the time. If we don't find the mast on the next dive or two, we should wait. We can always come back tomorrow."

"OK," Mike said. "Let's go out another 50 yards and try again. If we don't find it, we can head back to the beach."

Carol moved the raft while they hung on. Then Ed and Mike pushed away and let themselves sink below the surface. They each wore lead weights to keep from floating. They could stop and hang in the water at any spot they wanted. They did this by letting a bit of air into their wet suits. A kick of a fin was all it took to make them move when they wanted to. Each had a strong light. If the mast was near, they would find it.

Mike felt Ed's hand on his arm. He turned to see what Ed wanted. Ed pointed with his light. There in front of them, less than ten feet away, was the ship's mast.

Ed pointed at the center of his chest, then down. They couldn't talk underwater, but it was clear what he meant. Ed was going to go down. Mike moved his head up and down to show he understood.

Ed pushed away from Mike and headed down. He was following the mast, shining his light in front of him. Mike gave a kick of his fins and was right behind him.

Soon the rear part of the ship was in sight. It was bigger than it had seemed. And it was covered with dark brown rust and ocean plants. It had been on the bottom a long time.

Ed waved for Mike to follow him. Then he headed for the back of the ship. He pulled off some of the plants and rubbed the rusted metal on the back of the ship. Soon they could see some letters on the metal. They were able to make out the ship's name: *Demeter Star.*

Mike wanted to stay down and look around some more. But Ed pointed to his watch: They had been down long enough. It was time to go back up.

Ed finned back to the mast. Holding onto it, he headed slowly up. Mike followed. He remembered the rule Ed had taught him—never go up faster than your air bubbles are going up.

It took longer to get back to the surface than it had taken to reach the ship. Finally, they broke the surface and looked for Carol. The raft was about 100 yards to their left. They swam to it and pulled themselves up.

Mike was smiling from ear to ear. "We found it!" he said. "Not only that, we were able to read its name."

"What was it?" Carol asked.

"The *Demeter Star,*" Mike answered. "Have you ever heard of it?"

Carol shook her head. Then she turned to Ed. "Does that ring any bells with you?"

"No, it doesn't," Ed said. He didn't look happy.

"What's wrong?" Mike asked. "There could be a treasure down there."

"That's possible," Ed said. "But don't hold your breath until you find it."

"Why not?"

"Because I never heard of the *Demeter Star.*"

"So?"

"So, I've lived around here most of my life. If a ship with a rich cargo had gone down, I'd at least have heard the name."

"Maybe the sinking was a long time ago," Mike said.

"Oh, it *was* a long time ago. I can tell that much from the way the ship looks. But even so, I think I would have heard of the *Demeter Star.* I would have if it had anything of real worth on it when it went down."

"I hope you're wrong," Mike said.

"So do I," Carol said.

"That makes three of us," Ed told them.

Ed marked the spot with a wood float tied to a line. Then they turned the raft around and started rowing.

"OK, now what do we do?" Mike asked.

"You can take the next step all by yourself," Ed said. "In the morning, you can go to the Coast Guard Station. Maybe they can tell you something about the *Demeter Star.*"

CHAPTER **5**
123°W, 38°30′N

Lieutenant Kramer rubbed his nose. He was a short, blond man with a red face. "No, I never heard of the *Demeter Star*. But that doesn't mean anything. There are a lot of things I never heard of." Kramer was a new man at the Coast Guard Station.

"Is there a record of the ships that have gone down around here?" Mike asked.

"Let me check," Kramer said. He got up and left the room.

Mike sat and looked at pictures of Coast Guard ships that hung on the walls. Ten minutes went by, then ten more. Finally, Kramer returned with a thick book in his arms.

"Sorry to be so long," Kramer said. "Even with three men looking, it took a while."

"But you found something?" Mike asked.

"Sure did," Kramer said, dropping the book onto the center of his desk. He opened it to a page that was yellow with age and pointed with his finger. "Take a look at this."

Mike moved close. The writing had turned brown. But it could still be read:

DEMETER STAR, Seattle, Wash.—Sinking January 23, 1918—123° W, 38°30′N—n/h/n

"What's that say?" Mike asked.

"It's a record of the sinking of the *Demeter Star*. It gives the ship's home city and tells what happened to it. It gives someone's guess about where the ship went down. And it gives the date it happened. The last few letters mean that it isn't where it can cause trouble for other ships."

Mike made a face. "That isn't much of a record. It says almost nothing."

"Oh, this isn't the only record. This is just the day log. It was the best place to start. Now that we know the date of the sinking, we can find out more. I have a man checking now."

A few minutes later, one of Kramer's men brought them more about the *Demeter Star*. Because much of it wasn't clear to Mike, Kramer went through the records. As he read, he called out the important things.

"The *Demeter Star* ran into a winter storm," Kramer said. "The ship broke open and went under in minutes." Kramer turned a few more pages. Then he said, "It must have been really bad weather. Only three men lived to tell what happened."

"What was the ship carrying?" Mike asked.

"There is nothing here about its cargo," Kramer said. "As long as the cargo didn't cause the ship to sink, the Coast Guard wouldn't care what it was."

Mike didn't say anything for a few seconds. Then he asked, "Where can I find out what was on the ship?"

"That should be easy," Kramer said. "Go to the library."

"The library?"

"Yes, a library that has old newspapers. A newspaper story will tell you what was on the ship. It will probably tell you a lot of other things, too."

"Thanks. I'll try that." Mike turned to go.

"Say?" Kramer called, stopping him. "Why are you so interested in the *Demeter Star?* You haven't found it by any chance?"

"Yes, as a matter of fact, I did," Mike said. "It's under almost a hundred feet of water."

"And you think that old cargo ship may have something worth a lot of money on it? After all these years?"

"Well, I *hope* it does," Mike said. "So far I haven't learned for sure that it doesn't."

"Good luck to you," Kramer said. "You'll probably need all the luck you can get."

"Doesn't everyone?" Mike said.

Mike left the Coast Guard Station and went to the library. He spent an hour there, then went to Merek's Marine Market.

Ed and Carol came to him as soon as he walked through the door. "What did you find out?" Carol asked.

Mike told them about his visit to the Coast Guard Station. "Then I went to the library in Elk City," he said.

"What did you learn?" Ed asked.

"The ship was carrying fruit," Mike said. "Oranges. Back in those days, they didn't have many good roads. A lot of things that are sent by truck today were sent by ship in 1918. It was the quick way to move things from one place to another. The *Demeter Star* was taking a cargo of oranges from Los Angeles to Seattle when it went down."

"You don't seem very sad to find that out," Ed said.

Mike smiled. "Oh, I would rather the ship had been full of gold. But I found out it had something almost as good."

"*What?*" Carol and Ed both asked.

"Silver," Mike answered. "There was $20,000 in silver in the safe."

"That *is* good news," Ed said.

"But I have some bad news, too," Mike said. "Captain Gowers took some of the silver with him when he left the ship."

"How much?" Carol asked.

"No one knows," Mike told her. "His life boat turned over. Both he and the silver were lost. But anything he didn't take is still down there in the ship's safe."

"Well, then, there is only one way to find out what was left behind," Ed said.

"What's that?" Carol asked.

"We are going to have to go down and take a look," Ed said.

CHAPTER **6**

WE HAVE A PROBLEM

"OK, Ed, what do we do first?" Mike asked.

"I'll tell you what we *don't* do first. We don't tell anyone that we found the *Demeter Star*."

"I already told Lieutenant Kramer at the Coast Guard Station," Mike said.

"That can't be helped. It's done. The main thing now is that we don't tell anyone else. Did Kramer act like he thought you had found something important?"

"No. I got the idea he thought I was out of my mind. Diving down to an old cargo ship in a hundred feet of water. Something only a nut would do. Like that."

"Let's hope he keeps thinking that way. If he does, he won't say anything about it to any other divers."

"So, what's the plan?" Carol asked.

"We have to look that ship over and find the best way to get into it," Ed said. "That's going to take some study."

"We can take turns," Carol said. "While two of us are in the water, the other one can rest on the raft."

"Right," Mike said. "That way we never dive alone. And if anything goes wrong in the water, the one in the raft can help."

"That's the idea," Ed said. "I think I'll close the store until we're finished. As soon as I get a few more lights and lines together we will have everything we need."

Ed Merek's raft was meant to hold as many as six people. There was plenty of room for the three of them and all their equipment. Mike and Ed rowed out from White Rock Point. This time they found the right spot without trouble. The marker Ed had left was easy to spot.

"Mike and I will go down first," Ed said to Carol. "We will each have a long line tied to our waists. When we go inside the ship, the lines will tell you if we need help. They will also show us the way out again."

Mike and Ed got into the water. Soon all Carol could see were their air bubbles breaking the surface. The ends of the lines were tied to the raft. If Mike or Ed got into trouble, he would pull on the line to let her know.

They weren't gone long. Soon their heads popped out of the water beside her. Ed pushed up his mask. "We have a problem," he said.

Mike stayed in the water. He hung onto the side of the raft.

"What's the trouble?" Carol asked.

"That ship is sitting on the edge of an underwater cliff. Right on the edge. It could slip over at any time. Into maybe 400 or 500 feet of water."

"It has been there since 1918," Mike said. "And it hasn't fallen over yet."

"All we know is that it has been down there since 1918," Ed said. "How long it has been on the edge of that cliff is anyone's guess. There is no telling how much that ship moves in bad weather."

"Well, we can't move it away from the cliff, can we?" Mike asked.

"No. But going inside the ship is going to be bad enough. With the chance of the thing falling over the edge, it's worse. And we have to hurry. We don't want it to fall before we get to look inside the safe."

"I'd like to see the ship," Carol said.

"Go down with Mike while I check over the equipment," Ed said. He removed the line from his waist and gave it to her.

Carol got into the water beside Mike. Mike led the way. He used the ship's mast to show him where to go. He followed it down. The deeper they went, the less light there was. Soon they were in a dark, blue-gray world. They had to turn on their lights.

When they were floating above the ship, Mike pointed to the cliff. It was easy to see why he had missed seeing it before. It was so dark down there, they were lucky to be able to see the ship. Besides, the ship was all they had been looking for.

Carol kicked her fins and went to the rear of the ship. She pointed her light at the name. Then she went down toward the edge of the cliff. She looked over the edge for a few seconds. It just dropped off into black ocean water. The bottom could have been another 500 feet down. Or a thousand. She turned around and finned back toward Mike.

Mike pointed to his watch and then up. Carol moved her head up and down.

Mike finned toward the mast. When he reached it, he slowed. Carol grabbed his arm to stop him. A large, dark shape was cutting through the water above them. It moved away, but came right back.

This time it wasn't so far away. The light in Mike's hand shook as he pointed it. The thing was too large and too close for there to be any mistake.

It was a 25-foot great white shark!

Suddenly, Mike felt very cold.

CHAPTER **7**

SHARK!

The large man eater circled ten feet from them. Then it turned away. But it didn't go far. Soon it was back for another look.

When it had gone by the second time, Mike wanted to race to the surface. The only thing that stopped him was Carol's hand on his arm. He turned to her and she moved her head from side to side.

That was just great! The only thing he could think to do was the wrong thing.

Carol still held him by the arm. She was frightened, too. But she knew they had to use their heads. She tried to think of the best thing to do. She had met sharks in the water before. But never one this big. Or this hungry-looking.

The shark was coming back for another look. Its mouth was open and Mike could see its rows and rows of teeth. Mike didn't move. He was afraid it would soon decide it wanted them for breakfast or lunch. Mike didn't want to help it make up its mind.

This was no good. No good at all. They couldn't stay where they were. Even if the shark wouldn't come after them unless they tried to swim to the surface, they were in trouble. They were in a hundred feet of water. They would have to go up soon or they could get the bends. They couldn't try to wait out the shark. If they did, they would end up as dead as they would by rushing away.

That left only one thing—a *slow* escape.

Carol made a sign for Mike to get behind her. Then she moved so that the mast was between her and the shark. They began to swim toward the surface, slowly. They kept the mast between them and the shark every inch of the way. Every time the shark made a pass at them, they moved around the mast to keep it between them.

So far, so good. But thinking ahead, Mike saw a problem with Carol's plan. How would they get across the last 20 feet of water? There would be no mast to hide behind. Mike couldn't find an answer. He wondered if Carol had one.

Then the shark seemed to have made up its mind. The best way to find out if Mike and Carol were good to eat was to taste them. It came towards them with great speed, mouth open. They slipped out of its way just in time. The shark had to turn to keep from running into the mast.

Mike and Carol kept swimming toward the surface. But they were careful not to go faster than the bubbles from their mouth pieces.

The shark turned and came toward them again. And again, Mike and Carol got out of the way in time. Only now, Carol reached out and tried to hit the shark in the eye. And she dropped the light she used to hit it. The light went spinning away toward the ocean floor.

The shark turned again. But this time it didn't come after Mike and Carol. It headed down, following the light.

Now they were near the top of the mast. The surface was only 20 feet away. Should they take a chance and hope the shark would be busy with the light long enough for them to reach the raft? It was a big chance.

Mike didn't see what else they could do. He led the way to the raft without looking back. Then as soon as Carol was out of the water he pulled himself up beside her.

Mike took his mask off and sat catching his breath. Carol said one word, "Shark!" then did the same.

Ed looked like a kid who had bitten into a piece of fruit and found half a worm. "I'm glad you didn't pull on your lines to tell me you were in trouble. I wouldn't have wanted to come between you and your friend."

"Quick," Mike said. "Tell me again about the joys of scuba diving. I'm starting to forget."

"Me, too," Carol said.

"And shouldn't we start rowing?" Mike added. "That shark could put its teeth right through this raft."

"That's why we're better off just sitting here. Sharks are funny."

"It's all I can do to keep from laughing," Mike said to his friend.

"I mean, they are strange," Ed said. "They can feel a diver moving in the water. To them, it's like a fish that's in trouble and the sharks come to look. If we start to row, it may be the same as ringing a dinner bell for that shark."

"Then let's wait a l-o-n-g time before we start to row," Mike said.

"What kind of shark was it?" Ed asked.

"Big!" Mike said.

"It was a great white shark," Carol said. "It looked about a mile long."

"I didn't see how long it was," Mike said. "I couldn't take my eyes off its teeth. *They* were long enough."

"I was afraid we might run into a shark or two," Ed said.

"You knew there were sharks around here?" Mike asked in surprise.

"I knew there probably were. We're not too far from the mouth of a river. Sharks like to hang around river mouths and wait for food to come floating along. But with any kind of luck we never would have seen one."

"We had luck, all right—bad. Now what do we do? We can't look for the silver with a shark in the way," Mike said.

"Oh, sure we can," Ed told him. "We just have to move it out of the way. I have some shark sticks back at the store. We will each carry one of them from now on."

"Shark sticks?" Mike said. "What are they?"

"A shark stick is a long pole that gives sharks a bad jar when you touch them with it. They don't like to be hurt. It makes them stay away."

After waiting half an hour, they rowed to the beach. Ed got the shark sticks from the store. Then he came back to where Mike and Carol were waiting for him. He showed them how the shark sticks worked, and they returned to the spot over the ship.

"You and I will make the next dive," Ed told Mike. "Are you ready?"

"Wouldn't you rather take Carol?" Mike said, but he didn't really mean it. He was reaching for his air tank when he said it.

Mike followed Ed into the water and down to the mast. They stopped at the top of the mast for a few seconds and looked all around. No sharks. That made Mike feel better. The shark stick didn't seem like much to use against a great white shark. He hoped he would never have to put it to a test.

Ed pointed down and then led the way. Mike stayed close behind him. If another great white shark showed up, he wanted to be able to follow Ed's lead there, too.

On the way to the *Demeter Star* Mike saw a lot of fish. There were several he would have liked to eat, but not one was big enough to eat him. That was the way he wanted it to stay.

Ed stopped beside an opening in the side of the ship. He pulled down more line from above. He wanted to be sure there was enough to reach inside the ship. Mike did the same. Then Ed moved through the opening. Mike was right behind him again.

The inside of the ship was black. They could not have seen anything without their lights.

Hundreds and hundreds of small fish had been hiding there. As they moved deep into the insides of the ship, the fish hurried away from them and their lights.

In some places the metal walls had been rusted paper thin. But most of the ship was still strong. They came to a door. Ed pushed it open and went through. Mike gave a kick of his fins and went after him. He got caught on something and pushed with his foot against the side of the door. He was able to pull free, but his air hose caught on a piece of sharp metal. When he pulled, the metal cut the hose in two. Mike saw the rush of air bubbles.

And he tasted water in his mouth.

He had no air.

He couldn't live without air.

In another minute, he would drown.

CHAPTER **8**

SUMMER STORM

There was only one thing Mike could do. He had to find Ed. And he had to do it quick. He pointed his light at Ed's line and followed it. If Ed had stopped to wait for him, Mike might get out of this OK. If not . . . well, he couldn't waste time thinking about that.

He swam through a room filled with dirty water. He followed Ed's line down a long hall and into a side room. His chest hurt so much he wanted to scream. Then he ran into Ed.

Mike gave the sign Ed had taught him to use—"*I need air!*"

Ed took the air hose from his own mouth and gave it to Mike. Mike took two deep breaths, then gave the hose back to Ed. They took turns breathing from Ed's tank.

Ed gave a sign for Mike to come with him. Together, they returned the way they had

come. They used the trail made by their lines to show them the way.

Once outside the ship, they used the one tank to breathe all the way to the surface. When their heads popped out of the water, they both started talking at the same time.

"Now I know why—" Mike started.

"How did you—" Ed began.

"—no one should ever dive alone," Mike finished.

"—cut your air hose?" Ed completed.

Then they both laughed. They swam to the raft and pulled themselves onto it.

"What are you two so happy about?" Carol wanted to know. "Didn't you see any sharks?"

"Sharks?" Mike said, as if he had never heard the word before. "I forgot all about them."

"Well," Ed said. "I think we should forget about diving, too. For the rest of today, that is. We've had enough diving for one day."

"That's the best idea I've heard all week," Mike said.

Having a great white shark show an interest in him was bad. But running out of air at a hundred feet wasn't any fun, either. When both happen in the same day, anyone would have reason to stop diving for good. But not Mike.

At eight o'clock the next morning, Mike, Ed, and Carol were back on the raft.

"So far, you've made every dive," Ed told Mike. "It's your turn to sit up here and watch the lines."

"OK," Mike said. "I need a little more time to talk myself into diving again."

Ed pointed to the dark sky. "There is a storm moving in. It may not be long before you'll wish you were with Carol and me. Being pounded by heavy waves can be pretty bad."

"I thought it never rained in California in the summer," Mike said.

"It's been a funny year for weather," Carol answered. "This is the second summer storm we have had."

Ed and Carol put on their equipment. By the time they were ready, there was a strong wind and rain was falling. They tied lines to their waists and went into the water. Each carried a shark stick and a light.

Because of the dark sky, they needed their lights at once. Without them, they might not have found the mast.

As before, they followed the mast down to the *Demeter Star*. When they got close to the ship, it became hard to see again. Now their lights didn't help them much. The storm had dirtied the water near the ocean floor. It was lifting up the bottom mud. Ed and Carol could see almost nothing until they got into the ship.

Ed led the way, but stopped just inside the opening. There was room for only one diver at a time. Ed gave Carol a sign to wait where she was. He would go on alone first. He handed her his line to hold. By passing it through her fingers, she would be able to see that he had enough and that it didn't get caught on anything. Also, she would be able to feel him pull on it if he got into trouble.

Ed went on alone. He followed the same trail he and Mike had gone down the day before. Soon he was in front of the ship's safe. The door was open a bit, but not far enough for him to reach inside. It took everything he had to pull it open. Then, as he was putting his arm into it, the ship seemed to jump under him.

The next thing he knew, the ship was rolling onto its side.

And the safe was falling toward him.

Carol felt the ship start to move. She was able to swim through the opening and get out of it just in time. But she didn't let go of Ed's line. She was still holding it when the ship turned onto its side like a sleeping giant. A wave of mud and dirt washed over her. She knew her light was on, but she could not see it. She swam up, trying to find clear water, but there wasn't any.

Then there were several sharp pulls on the line. Ed was telling her he was in trouble.

Carol stopped worrying about the dirty water that was thick all around her. Using touch instead of sight, she followed the line. Once she was inside the ship, the water cleared a bit. But it was still hard to see very much even with her light.

She had to move old boxes and rusted equipment out of her way. They were blocking doors. Then she reached Ed. The ship's safe had fallen over and his leg was pinned under it. The open safe door held the safe up a few inches. If it hadn't, Ed's leg would have been smashed flat when the safe had fallen.

Carol pushed against the safe, but it would not move. It was much too heavy for her to lift.

She knew she had to do something—and do it fast. Ed's air would not last much longer. She needed help.

Carol pulled at both their lines several times. Then she felt an answering pull from above. Then nothing. Mike was on his way.

I hope he follows the lines, she thought. *If he doesn't, he will get lost in the black water and never find us.*

The minutes seemed like hours. She was sure it was taking Mike too long to find them. He must have gotten lost in the dark, dirty water. She was thinking of leaving Ed to look for Mike when Mike got there.

All the trouble they had had seemed to have made Mike strong. When he saw what had happened, he didn't need to be told what to do. He went to Ed and looked at the way his leg was pinned. Then he checked Ed's air tank to see how full it was. Next he checked Carol's tank.

Ed had much less air than Carol. He had used it up trying to free himself. Before Mike could even think about how he might get the safe off him, he had to give him more air.

But how?

CHAPTER **9**

THE SAFE

Then, suddenly, Mike knew what he had to do. He took off his air tank and gave it to Ed. Then he let Carol know that they would both have to use her tank.

Together, Mike and Carol swam to the opening in the side of the ship. They took turns breathing from Carol's mouth piece as they went. There, Mike made it clear that she should stay below and help Ed while he went back to the raft for more air. They had several full tanks on it.

The trouble was, he would have to make the return to the raft without air.

Not only that, he would have to go slowly, no faster than his air bubbles. Bubbles it was too black to see. If he went up too fast, gas bubbles would form in his blood. That would either kill him or keep him from helping Ed.

Mike took a couple of deep breaths. Then he gave Carol back her mouth piece. He kept his light, but let his shark stick drop. If he ran into a shark, the stick wouldn't save him. He wouldn't have enough air to take the time to use the stick. Besides, the way the water was, he couldn't see a shark.

Mike started for the surface. As he went slowly up, he kept letting air out of his lungs, a little at a time. He watched the bubbles float up. It seemed he would never reach the surface. One minute passed. Then two. He thought his lungs were on fire.

Mike thought he could hold his breath no longer. He needed air! His whole body was crying for air. But he forced himself to go slowly. Now he could see the surface. But could he make it? At last his head popped above the surface.

Air never smelled so good. Never! He rested there, catching his breath. Even the strong wind and rain couldn't bother him. Then he swam to the waiting raft.

There were four air tanks on it. He put one on and tied the other three together. Then, so he could get them back if he dropped them, he tied the other end of the line to his waist.

He forced himself to rest a few minutes. He felt like he could fall asleep right there in the storm. The trip to the surface without an air tank had taken a lot out of him. He was very tired. And his lungs still burned.

But he had to go back down. If he didn't, Ed and Carol would never get to the surface alive. Both of them needed air. And there was no one else to get the safe off Ed's leg. The lives of his friends were in Mike's hands.

He put the tanks into the water and slipped over the side. He followed Ed and Carol's lines. The lines would take him right to them.

Mike followed the lines down. The air tanks were easy to handle in the water. Their weight was less than it was on the surface. Mike was happy about that. He wished there were some way he could make the weight of the safe less. Then he could move it off Ed's leg.

Down, down he went through the black water. His light was no help at all. He carried it because he would need it inside the ship.

Then he came to the end of the lines.

But he was not in the ship.

And Ed and Carol were not there.

The lines were caught between two rocks on the bottom. The ship had moved again while he was on the raft. It might have fallen off the underwater cliff deep onto the ocean floor. If it did, Ed and Carol were gone for good.

Then he heard a sound. It was not very loud. It was like someone far away was hitting a drum. He listened, trying to tell which way the sound was coming from. It seemed to be coming from the right.

Mike swam toward the sound. Ed and Carol were the only ones down there who could be making the sound. They had to be doing it to let him know where they were.

Sure enough. There was the ship. He almost swam into its side. Mike had to hunt to find the opening. Then he went inside.

He found Carol in the room where Ed was pinned. She was sitting on the floor beside Ed. She was pounding on the side of the ship with her empty air tank. They were both breathing from the tank Mike had left.

Mike gave them each a fresh tank. Then he took a look at the way Ed was held by the safe.

When the ship had moved, the safe had crashed down, catching Ed's leg. The open safe door had held one end up so that his leg wasn't broken. But he could not pull it free. And the safe was too heavy for Ed to lift.

Mike got down where he could reach through the open space beside Ed's leg. He felt the leg to be sure it was not broken. If he could get the safe to move, Ed would be able to swim away. He made a sign to Carol, asking her to help lift. Ed helped from where he was. The three of them used all the power they had.

And the heavy safe stayed right where it was.

CHAPTER **10**

MORE THAN NOTHING

Mike remembered how light the air tanks had been underwater. And he knew he didn't have the same weight he had on the surface. Why wasn't the safe lighter, too? Was there anything he could do to make it lighter?

Suddenly, he knew the answer. He and the tanks were lighter because they were taking up the space of water that would have more weight than they did.

But what if the safe were full of air instead of water . . . ?

That was the answer!

Mike took the last tank of air and pushed the end of it into the opening beside Ed's leg. Then he opened the tank. Air rushed out of it and into the open safe. Because the open door was facing down, the air took the place of the water that was in the safe.

When air started coming out of the safe, he knew it was as full as he could make it. Again he let Carol know he wanted her to help. And again all three of them pushed and pulled at the safe with all their might.

This time the safe lifted. Not much, but just enough to let Ed pull his leg free.

However, the ship was moving again. The sound of it sliding over rock filled the ship.

With Mike leading the way, they finned through the old ship. They left empty tanks and shark sticks behind. They took only the light Mike had. All they wanted to save was their lives. Nothing else mattered.

Mike reached the opening to the ocean and went through. Carol and Ed followed him out. Behind them, the ship slid over the underwater cliff. They hadn't left it a second too soon.

The *Demeter Star* was gone forever.

Now they had the problem of getting to the surface again. Much as they all would have liked to hurry, they knew they had to go slowly. After all they had been through, no one wanted to get the bends. Or worse.

They held hands and took a long time going up. They felt very close to each other. After what they had been through, they would always feel close.

This time when they broke the surface, there was no shouting. They made no noise at all. They swam to the raft and climbed onto it without a word. They had passed the worst time of their lives without words. Now that it was over, they didn't need them.

Mike rowed for a while, then Carol took over. The storm was moving away. When they reached the beach, they pulled the raft out of the water and left it. Side by side, they walked to the van. Carol drove it to Ed's beach house and they went inside.

Mike was the first to speak. "I guess there wasn't any silver left in the safe after all," he said. He sounded very tired.

"That's right. Captain Gowers must have taken all the silver with him," Ed said.

"Then it was for nothing," Carol said. "We were almost killed for nothing. And we lost the air tanks and other equipment for nothing. It doesn't seem fair."

"What do you mean, it doesn't *seem* fair?" Mike asked. "You don't sound sure."

"All right," Carol said. "It *isn't* fair."

"That's more like it," Mike said slowly. "We did it all for nothing, and that's not fair."

Ed smiled. "We got more than nothing," he said slowly.

"We did?" Mike looked surprised. "What?"

Ed dug into the tiny pocket of his wet suit. "While my leg was caught under the safe, I had plenty of time to feel around. I saw there were a lot of these things by the safe."

Ed brought out some small, gray stones. A few were not much bigger than the head of a nail. Others were as big around as ten cent pieces. He made a pile of them in the center of the kitchen table.

Mike picked up a few of them. He rubbed them between his fingers.

Ed went on. "There was probably a small package of them in the ship's safe. When the ship went down, they were not seen. Maybe there was nothing on the package to tell what was in it. Later, the package went to pieces in the water. And when the safe fell over, they rolled out."

Carol picked up some of the stones, too.

"I don't know why there was nothing in that newspaper story at the library about them," Ed finished.

"What are you talking about?" Mike said.

"These rocks," Ed said. "Don't you know what they are?"

Mike said, "They feel like they have oil on them."

"They always feel that way," Ed said. "That's how I knew what they were."

"Ed Merek," Carol said. "Stop playing with us. Tell us what you're talking about."

"Diamonds," Ed said.

"These don't look like diamonds," Carol said.

"That's because they haven't been cut yet. They will after they have been cut."

"Diamonds?" Mike said. "You're sure?"

"I'm sure. I've seen them before."

"What do you think they are worth?" Mike asked.

"I can't say for sure, but they are worth a lot. More than the silver, I'll bet."

Mike and Carol stood with their mouths open. Slowly they began to smile. Then all three of them were laughing.

Some people going by on the beach heard them. They thought a party was going on.

They were right.